An Introduction to Self-Directed Study

Anne Murdoch BSc (Hons) PGCE PhD MIMgT
Professor and Head of School of Community Studies
City College, Norwich

Bryn Davies BA (Hons) ALA DMS MIInfSc MIMgT
Senior Lecturer
City College, Norwich

Scutari Press · London

© Scutari Press 1994

Scutari Press is a division of Scutari Projects Ltd., the publishing company of the Royal College of Nursing.

First published 1994

British Library Cataloguing in Publication Data

Murdoch, Anne
  Introduction to Self-directed Study
  I. Title II. Davies, Bryn
  371.3028

  ISBN 1-871364-69-8

Typeset by Dorwyn Ltd, Rowlands Castle, Hants
Printed and bound in Great Britain by
Hobbs the Printers of Southampton

CONTENTS

1   Introduction 1

2   Self-directed learning 3

3   Forms of education 6

4   Self-directed learning in practice . . . 10

5   Planning your study 14

6   Literature searching 20

7   Referencing 28

8   Critically reviewing research reports . . 37

9   Writing reports 42

10   Developing a personal action plan . . . 45

11   Evaluating yourself 47

12   Bibliography 49

1 INTRODUCTION

This workbook is intended as an introduction to self-directed learning and research skills for the adult learner. It will be most effective in helping the student who is new to this type of learning to come to grips with the concept of self-directed study.

The workbook contains activities and self-assessment questions.

SELF-ASSESSMENT QUESTIONS

Each self-assessment question (SAQ) will help you decide how much you have understood about the section and what you will need to go over again.

ACTION

Each activity is intended to build upon the previous one and provide a basis for the next activity. It may come in the form of action or a self-assessment question. Because the activities link together, it is important that you attempt each one. The activities are an important way for you to decide how well you are doing and whether you need to go over parts of the text again.

2 SELF-DIRECTED LEARNING

What does self-directed learning mean to you?

Self-directed learning is a method by which a person takes an active part in his or her learning, either in addition to a planned course or as a central part of it.

Self-directed learning is different from either:

- *flexible learning*, which involves different modes of learning on a course of study. This may include learning packages, taught courses and video packages as part of the programme;

  or

- *open learning*, which gives the student open access to education. Individuals can study individual learning packages or parts of programmes as they wish;

  or

- *distance learning,* which involves the individual following study packages, usually in their own home and away from a student centre. Usually some tutorial support, either by telephone or by attendance at a centre, is available.

Self-directed learning involves individuals in taking a central role in directing and managing their own learning. They may negotiate learning objectives or outcomes with a teacher or mentor and actively plan their own course of study, its content, background reading and research. A self-directed learner is one who knows what he or she wants to study and what learning outcomes he or she wishes to achieve.

YOU

People learn in a variety of ways, and for this to be most effective, they need to identify for themselves how best they can learn and how to motivate themselves and have self-confidence. There are a large number of texts available to help you find out how people learn. Ask your librarian to direct you to what is available in your local library. Section 3 below may help you to think about how you learn new skills.

THE TEACHER

Teachers can be instructors, advisors, enablers and facilitators, but should not just attempt to control what the student learns. Students need to be able to grow and mature at their own pace, to find out new information for themselves and to take responsibility for their own learning.

YOU AND THE TEACHER

You can help yourself and your teacher by giving feedback on what you find easy or difficult to learn and how you have learnt best in the past.

The basic philosophy of self-directed learning is that:

Learning does not equate with teaching; i.e. individuals do not only learn by being taught, they also learn by discovering for themselves.

Research relating to self-directed learning (Jarvis, 1985) suggests that self-directed learners are more likely to:

- sustain motivation and enthusiasm;
- stimulate thought;
- combat dissatisfactions;
- believe in themselves and their ability to learn.

SAQ

What is self-directed learning, and how does it differ from open learning, distance learning and flexible learning?

_____

_____

_____

_____

_____

_____

_____

3 FORMS OF EDUCATION

There are two fundamental forms of education according to Jarvis (1985). These are **pedagogy** and **andragogy**.

Pedagogy is the science of teaching, and is referred to as education from above.

Andragogy is the science of helping adults to learn, and is referred to as education of equals.

Education from above (Pedagogy)		Education of equals (Andragogy)
	Definitives	
Teacher as director responsible for learning		Learner responsible for own learning
	OBJECTIVE	
Student is moulded to fit into system		Student grows and matures irrespective of the system
	Role	
Passive		Active
	Assessment	
Examination		Self/peer assessment

The implication of the above is that learners and teachers need to understand a range of methods of learning in order to appreciate the implications of self-directed learning.

▬▬▬▬▬ ACTION

Each person learns through a range of strategies, i.e. access to information via a number of different routes.

Make a list of different ways one may acquire knowledge and learn.

_____

_____

_____

_____

_____

_____

_____

Your answers may have included some of the following:

- By rote (off by heart).
- Via a teacher or lecturer giving instructions.
- Observation, e.g. watching an 'expert', television or video.
- Participation, e.g. helping or 'trying a skill out'.
- Reading.
- Experience, e.g. picking up tips through practice.
- Trial and error.
- Shared knowledge, e.g. self-help groups.
- Computer-assisted learning.
- Listening.

■■■■ ACTION

This exercise is intended to help you to focus on how you learn. It builds upon the learning strategies of the previous page and is aimed at helping you to identify your strengths and weaknesses in relation to such strategies.

(1) Reflect on your past experience of learning and write down three learning experiences which you found:

  (a) **Valuable**

_____

_____

_____

_____

_____

_____

  (b) **Unhelpful (or disastrous)**

_____

_____

_____

_____

_____

_____

(2) Take one example from each answer and write down why the experience was valuable or unhelpful.

  (a) **Valuable**

_____

_____

_____

▶

_____

_____

_____

(b) **Unhelpful (or disastrous)**

_____

_____

_____

_____

_____

It may be helpful for you to go over some of the points we have discussed about self-directed learning and to think of the learning experiences you found valuable.

_____

_____

_____

_____

_____

_____

FURTHER READING

Apps JW (1982) *Study Skills for Adults Returning to School.* London: McGraw Hill.

Irving A (1982) *Starting To Teach Study Skills.* London: Edward Arnold.

4 SELF-DIRECTED LEARNING IN PRACTICE

This chapter provides the basis for reflection on the skills that are important in self-directed learning. By the end of the chapter, you should feel more confident about your own ability to plan your study.

■ ACTION

Draw up a list of the skills that you think are most important in developing a positive approach to directing your own learning. Please put these in order of priority below.

(1) _____

(2) _____

(3) _____

(4) _____

(5) _____

(6) _____

(7) _____

(8) _____

(9) _____

(10) _____

Your list may have included some of the priorities below.

- Confidence.
- Planning.
- Time management.
- Filing.
- Note taking.
- Report writing.
- Reading.
- Self-help groups.
- Identifying learning aims.
- Self-discipline.
- Communication.
- Application of theory to practice.
- Listening.
- Searching for information.

ACTION

Using the lines provided below, rewrite the above list in order of priority, according to what you feel are the most important skills. There is no right answer of course; the list depends on what is right for you.

_____

_____

_____

_____

_____

_____

_____

_____

_____

■ ACTION

The following exercise will help you to assess your own skill levels and where there may be room for improvement.

Complete the following exercise by ticking one column for each skill.

Do you have the ability to:	No 1	A little 2	A lot 3
Take instructions			
Concentrate			
Manage time			
Acquire information			
Read for comprehension			
Plan your learning			
Keep a filing system			
Take notes			
Write reports/essays			
Assist or support others			
Identify learning aims and objectives			
Be self-disciplined			
Listen skilfully			
Manage workloads			

▨ REFLECTION

Total up your responses: count 1 for 'No', 2 for 'A little', and 3 for 'A lot'. If you scored 31–42, you are already very competent as a learner. If you scored 18–30, you will need to work on the 14 skill areas and may wish to seek help from a tutor. If you scored below 18, you may feel you need quite a lot of improvement in study skills. Do not worry, because most adult learners feel they need help in these areas. A taught course of study skills may be helpful, and is available at many centres of education. You will find the names and telephone numbers of these in the local directories or at your local library.

Having completed the last two exercises, you should now have a better understanding of the types of skill that are needed for self-directed learning, and, if you have been honest with yourself, you will now be aware of the skill areas you need to pay particular attention to. This may mean that a little polishing is required, or you may need to seek further help in a particular skill.

With a greater understanding of the skills required for self-directed learning, you are now ready to apply those skills in planning your study programme.

5 PLANNING YOUR STUDY

Below are some points to consider in planning your study (i.e. self-directed study), whether you join a formal course or study on your own.

At the beginning of a course, you should consider three things:

- **What is to come?**
- **What commitment is expected of you?**
- **What commitment can you give?**

REMEMBER:

Avoid

Falling

Behind

With

Your

Study

You can do this by:

- having a strategy for study and setting yourself realistic targets and goals for which to aim;

- planning a realistic schedule for study allowing for the other commitments you have (e.g. domestic, work and holidays);

- Being flexible in your planning to take account of unpredictable factors such as illness.

GUIDELINES FOR PLANNING YOUR STUDY

- Scan your course information – can you do any work which will fit in with other commitments? e.g. an essay which fits in with a report that you have to do at work. This gives a sense of where you are going and how parts of a planned course can relate to your work.

- Read the aims and objectives of a course. What is expected of you? What new skills will you be expected to learn?

- Plan a schedule which will enable you to complete your coursework early without having to burn the midnight oil.

- Make time for additional reading.

- Do some work most days, even if only a little is fitted in between other activities.

- Monitor your own progress – this helps to motivate the individual learner.

- Try and find a quiet place at home where you can work without interruptions or distractions.

Other tips you might find useful are:

- Read, listen, discuss.
- Cut out newspaper articles.
- File your work.
- Keep full references in an index file for future use.

SAQ

What are the six basic guidelines for planning your study?

(1) _____

(2) _____

(3) _____

(4) _____

(5) _____

(6) _____

You should always be systematic and organised in your approach to study.

STUDY AND RESEARCH SKILLS

Self-directed study involves research of some kind, whether litera-ture searching or a research study. Many courses now expect their members to complete a project of some kind. The following check-list will help those who are doing research-based study and those who are doing projects as part of a course.

- Identify your own areas of interest and those relating to your work by asking yourself questions about what you find interesting, relevant or topical.

- Analyse your needs and priorities for learning.

  - What information do you need?

  - What would you like to know?

  - What might you like to know?

  - How and where can you get hold of the information you need?

- Identify the aims and objectives of your course of study.

  - What do you expect to get out of your course of study?

  - What do others expect to get out of it?

  - What would you like to get out of it?

- Plan the content and direction of study.

- Plan the sequence of learning or research. What do you need to do first in order to proceed with your study?

- Select any appropriate training methods you may need and seek out advice.

- Build a self-evaluation or appraisal mechanism into your work. Consider structure, process and outcome of the course of study. What is involved? What is expected? (Section 11 includes an action plan which may help to take this further.)

It is likely that at some stage in your studies you will be required to investigate a problem, read research reports or even undertake a small-scale study. The five steps below are the routes which a researcher will follow when undertaking a full research project, although you will not be expected to follow all five steps at this stage.

THE FIVE STEPS

Step 1 Plan research

(a) Decide the aims of the research and its focus.

(b) Carry out a literature search.

(c) Plan and design the research study and make it operational.

(d) Choose appropriate research methods for collecting and analysing data.

Step 2 Collect data

(a) Decide on the type of data you will need, i.e. from historical research, observational methods (conducting interviews), experimental methods (carrying out experiments) or developmental research (questionnaires, etc).

(b) Carry out fieldwork (collect information about the field of study).

Step 3 Collate and analyse data

(a) Data collation.

(b) Analysis of data (use of computers, statistics, etc.).

(c) Reference to aims and focus of research.

Step 4 Write report

Write the report, giving the presentation of your findings, your conclusion and interpretation of the results and (if possible) your recommendations.

Step 5 Disseminate information

Disseminate and publish the results.

Section 6 moves on to the topic of literature searching, and the rest of this workbook is designed to help you understand what skills are required in undertaking research. This should be of benefit whether you are to undertake a small piece of work or critically read research reports. Once you have a clear idea of what research involves, you will be better able to read and criticise others' research.

6 LITERATURE SEARCHING

Literature searching is the first and arguably the most vital stage in the research process. The main reason for undertaking a literature search is to discover what has been written on a particular topic, and by which author(s).

As with all parts of research, it is important to plan your search to save wasting time. Before beginning your search you should ask yourself three questions:

What? Where? How?

WHAT INFORMATION DO I NEED?

Write down all the subject areas you want to research. Break your subject down into 'keywords', and list possible synonyms, e.g. cot death, sudden infant death syndrome, SIDS.

Decide what sort of information you want, e.g. historical, scientific, social or economic.

WHERE AM I GOING TO GET THE INFORMATION?

A nursing or hospital library is the obvious answer, but other sources may be available for use, such as public, college and university libraries.

You will need to establish some of the following.

- How do I use the library?

- What are the opening hours of the library?

- Does it have the necessary information?

- Are the items available for loan?

- Is it quiet?

- Are refreshments available nearby?

- Can I obtain items not held in the library?

HOW WILL I FIND THE INFORMATION I NEED?

The most important step is to consult the librarian. He or she will be able to tell you where to find the information, how to use the catalogues and various indexes, and whether the information you want is available at another library.

USING LIBRARIES

The overwhelming majority of libraries will have their book-stock catalogued, and in most cases this will have been computerised. If this is the case, ask one of the librarians to show you how the system works. The ability to search catalogues successfully and accurately will help you considerably in your search for information.

You will need to familiarise yourself with the layout of the library you intend to use and get to know where each section is. As well as from books, information may be obtained from:

- audiovisual material – videos, audiocassettes;

- pamphlets;

- local studies sections;

- project files;

- newspaper cuttings, etc.

You will also need to know the procedures in your library for reserving books that are on loan, ordering books that your library does not stock and getting access to computerised information.

■ ACTION

Find the library catalogue or subject indexes, and see if you can trace any information on one of the following subjects (remembering to list synonyms if applicable).

- Pregnancy.

- Health education.

- AIDS.

Jot down the shelf numbers and ask the librarian to give you a plan of the library or to explain the relevance of the numbers you have written down.

_____

_____

_____

_____

_____

Bibliographies (lists of books, journals, etc.) are available relating to literature on a wide range of subjects, and include:

- *Management: A selected bibliography* (Mason, 1992)

- *A Bibliography of Nursing Literature* (Walsh, 1985)

- *British National Bibliography* (British Library, 1950–)

These will list books (and occasionally other material) relating to a particular subject and give you an excellent start in your search for information. You will need to find out whether your library has any bibliographies in your subject area.

PERIODICALS

One of the best ways of obtaining information is through magazines, periodicals or newspapers.

Most libraries receive some periodicals, and you will need to know which ones are relevant to your research. The librarian will be able to tell you whether there is a list available of the periodicals the library receives, and whether it is alphabetical or broken down into subject areas. If it is broken down into subjects, you will be able to work from your keywords to see if any of the subjects are relevant to your study.

■■■■■■ ACTION

Does the library take any of the following:

- *Nursing Standard*
- *Health Visitor*
- *New Statesman & Society*

Make a few brief notes as to their potential usefulness.

_____

_____

_____

If you find that the library has a large number of titles, you will soon appreciate that to read through all the journals would be a tedious process, as very few have their own index. There are, however, some indexing and abstracting services which index a wide range of journals.

ABSTRACTS AND INDEXES

The Royal College of Nursing has a *Nursing Bibliography* (1972–) which indexes in excess of 300 nursing journals and can be a great time saver when seeking information on a particular topic.

There are a number of similar publications covering the nursing and health field, e.g.:

- *International Nursing Index* (ISSN 0020 8124)

- *Cumulative Index to Nursing and Allied Health Literature* (CINAHL) (ISSN 0416 5554)

- *Nursing Research Abstracts* (ISSN 0141 3899)

- *Applied Social Science Index and Abstracts* (ASSIA) (ISSN 0950 2238)

It is helpful to find out which publications are taken in your library. You may need to ask the librarian how to use these because they can be a little confusing at first sight.

The difference between an index and an abstract is that the abstract will give a summary of the contents of an article, whereas an index gives just the title. For example:

Nursing Bibliography

Alternative Medicine

Smith, M. Healing through touch. (Therapeutic touch) *Nursing Times* **86**, 24 Jan 1990, pp.31–32.

Applied Social Sciences Index and Abstracts (ASSIA)

NURSING: Therapeutic touch

Healing through touch. M Smith. *Nursing Times*, **86** (24 Jan 90) pp.31–32.

Believes that the therapeutic value of touch is not sufficiently appreciated. Describes how, as part of a project for a nursing degree, she explored its potential . . .

This is also a good example of how different indexes and abstracting services use different keywords to index the same article, and highlights the need to list synonyms when making a list of keywords for research.

■■■■■ ACTION

(1) Does your library stock any abstracting or indexing journals?

_____

_____

_____

_____

_____

_____

_____

(2) Using the keywords from the earlier exercise, can you find any references to them in these publications?

_____

_____

_____

_____

_____

_____

_____

_____

COMPUTERISED SEARCHING

To make the task of searching for information even simpler, many indexes and abstracts have now been computerised, and literature searches can be carried out using a computer. There are two principal ways in which these can be carried out:

- On-line searching.

- CD-ROM.

On-line searches are normally only carried out on your behalf by professional librarians, mainly because of the high costs of being on-line to another computer. Nevertheless, there are three very useful databases, CINAHL, MEDLINE and DHSS data, which cover the nursing and medical field. Ask a librarian whether these services can be accessed.

CD-ROMs, however, can usually be accessed by individuals and are normally free of charge, except possibly for printing out material. The most useful of these in the nursing field are CINAHL and ASSIA. You do not require any particular computer skills to be able to use these facilities, and from our experience, people very quickly pick up the routines necessary to retrieve information. It is very important to become familiar with CD-ROMs, if they are available, as they can save you hours of time in comparison with manual searching of indexes and catalogues.

OTHER SOURCES OF INFORMATION

Occasionally your search for information in your local library may prove to be fruitless. As you will have gathered, your library can order you material from other libraries. However, it may be more convenient and useful to visit a specialist library like that of the Royal College of Nursing.

Two publications which list libraries with special collections are *Aslib's Shorter Directory of Information Sources in the United Kingdom* (Codlin, 1986) and the *Directory of Medical and Health Care Libraries in the United Kingdom and the Republic of Ireland* (Wright, 1992).

Examples

If you were doing a project on Alzheimer's disease or cot death, and could not find enough information, the Aslib directory tells you that special library collections are available at the:

> Alzheimer's Disease Society (ADS)
> 158–60 Balham High Road
> London
> SW12 9BN

or

Foundation for the Study of Infant Death
(Cot Death Research and Support)
15 Belgrave Square
London
SW1X 8PS

Most of the listed organisations allow students to use their facilities, although not necessarily for borrowing.

The preceding pages have attempted to introduce you to the basic concepts of literature searching, and in no way claim to be comprehensive. It is, therefore, vitally important to ask librarians for assistance. Librarians (and information scientists) are highly trained professionals and may be able to help you in more ways than you realise.

7 REFERENCING

This chapter is intended as a brief introduction to referencing styles. The correct referencing of work is extremely important as it is academically elevating and allows the reader to check the sources on which to base an argument.

There are three principal styles of referencing (in accordance with British Standard 5605, British Standards Institution, 1990):

- The **name and date** (Harvard) system.
- The **Numeric** system (also known as the Vancouver system).
- The **Running notes** system.

The first and second are by far the most common. 'Running notes' is a rather more complex variety of the numeric system which is not recommended for those returning to learning and is not discussed in this book.

CITING REFERENCES IN THE TEXT

The name and date (Harvard) system

The name and date system, more commonly referred to as the Harvard system, involves citing the name(s) of the author(s) and date of publication as the references appear in the text. This can be done in two ways. If the author is mentioned in the text, the reference is cited as in example 1. If, however, the text is referring only to the author's work, the reference appears as in example 2.

Example 1

> Much recent practice in nursing and midwifery education is prone to cite the 'theory of andragogy' introduced by Lindeman (1926) and more recently Knowles (1975, 1978, 1980) and the 'person-centred approach' to learning identified by Rogers (1977, 1983).

Example 2

> Mothers have also expressed feelings of hopelessness and frustration during pain crises (Perrin & Maclean, 1988; Sabbeth & Leventhal, 1984), and need for social support (Midence et al, 1982; Abrams, 1987). These feelings were suggested to be a result of the family's susceptibility to psychosocial problems and the inability to cope with SCD (Graham et al, 1982; Capelli et al, 1989).

When citing a book or article which has two authors, it is common to cite both, e.g. (Perrin & Maclean, 1988), whereas if there are more than two authors, it is normal to cite the first author followed by 'et al', e.g. (Graham et al, 1982).

Occasionally an author will have a different item published in the same year, in which case one would differentiate by lower case letters, a b c, etc., e.g. (Bloom 1990a, 1990b).

The numeric system

Instead of using the author's name and date of publication, each reference is given a number as it appears in the text. The first reference cited will therefore always be number 1.

Example 3

> Much recent practice in nursing and midwifery education is prone to cite the 'theory of andragogy' introduced by Lindeman[15] and more recently Knowles[27,9,18] and the 'person-centred approach' to learning identified by Rogers[1,30].

Example 4

> Mothers have also expressed feelings of hopelessness and frustration during pain crises[5,6] and need for social support[8,10]. These feelings were suggested to be a result of the family's susceptibility to psychosocial problems and the inability to cope with SCD[12,13].

Note that the numeric system avoids the need to use multiple authors in the text (compare examples 2 and 4). The numeric system generally does not disturb the text as much as the Harvard system, although the latter gives the reader a feel as to the particular authors upon whom the argument is based.

Most students find the name and date (Harvard) system somewhat easier to use, although tutors normally give students guidelines on the type of referencing required.

WRITING FULL REFERENCES

Both the Harvard and numeric systems list the cited references in full at the end of the text. A full reference, as defined by the British Standards Institution (BSI, 1990), is as follows.

Reference to a book

| **Harvard** | Author | Knowles MS |
| | Date | 1978 |

	Title	Self directed learning: a guide for learners and teachers
	Place: Publisher	Chicago: Follett

Knowles MS (1978) *Self Directed Learning: a guide for learners and teachers.* Chicago: Follett.

Numeric	Author	Knowles MS
	Title	Self directed learning: a guide for learners and teachers
	Place: Publisher	Chicago: Follett
	Date	1978

Knowles MS. *Self Directed Learning: a guide for learners and teachers.* Chicago: Follett, 1978.

Reference to a contribution in a book

Harvard	Author	Zaremba Jacek
	Year	1985
	Title	Recent medical research
	Editors	Lane, David & Stratford, Brian
	Title	Current approaches to Down's Syndrome
	Place: Publisher	London: Cassell
	Pages	27–51

Zaremba, J (1985) Recent medical research. *In* Lane, David & Stratford, Brian. *Current Approaches to Down's Syndrome,* pp.27–51. London: Cassell.

Numeric	Author	Zaremba, Jacek
	Title	Recent medical research
	Editors	Lane, David & Stratford, Brian
	Title	Current approaches to Down's Syndrome
	Place: Publisher	London: Cassell
	Year	1985
	Pages	27–51

Zaremba J. Recent medical research. *In* Lane, David & Stratford, Brian. *Current Approaches to Down's Syndrome.* London: Cassell, 1985, pp.27–51.

Reference to a contribution in a journal or periodical

Harvard	Author	Barber, Phil
	Year	1992
	Title	Phobias
	Journal	Nursing Times
	Numbers	Volume 88. No 52. December 30
	Pages	22–24

Barber P (1992) Phobias. *Nursing Times.* Vol 88, No 52. December 30. pp. 22–24.

Numeric	Author	Barber, Phil
	Title	Phobias
	Journal	Nursing Times
	Numbers	Volume 88. No. 52. December 30 1992
	Pages	22–24

Barber P. Phobias. *Nursing Times.* Vol 88, No 52. December 30 1992. pp. 22–24.

The full references for both systems are listed at the end of the text. The Harvard is listed alphabetically and the numeric, as one would expect, numerically.

In the earlier examples 1 to 4, the references would look like this:

Harvard System

Abrams SJ (1987) The self concept of sickle cell disease and their siblings and related maternal attitudes. *Dissertation Abstracts International.* Vol 47, No 10. 3869.

Bird C & Hassall J (1993) *Self-administration of Drugs: a guide to implementation.* London: Scutari Press.

Cappelli M, McGrath PJ, MacDonald NE, Katsanis J & Lascelles M (1989) Parental care and overprotection of children with cystic fibrosis. *British Journal of Medical Psychology.* Vol 62, No 3. pp. 281–289.

Ghazi F & Cook S (1993) Monitoring research in a nursing college. *Nursing Standard.* Vol 7, No 47. pp. 27–30.

Graham AV, Reed KG, Levitt C, Fine M & Medalie JH (1982) Care of a troubled family and their child with sickle cell anemia. *Journal of Family Practice.* Vol 15, No 1. pp. 23–32.

Knowles MS (1975) *Self Directed Learning: a guide for learners and teachers.* Chicago: Follett.

Knowles MS (1978) *The Adult Learners: A Neglected Species.* 2nd edn. Houston: Gulf.

Knowles, MS (1980) *The Modern Practice of Adult Education: From Pedagogy to Andragogy.* Chicago: Follett.

Lindeman E (1926) *The Meaning of Adult Education.* New York: New Republic.

Midence K, Davies SC & Fuggle P (1992) Sickle cell disease: courage in the face of crisis. *Nursing Times.* Vol 88, No 22. pp. 46–48.

Pearce C (1993) Formal measurement of pain by nurses. *Nursing Standard.* Vol 7, No 21. pp. 38–39.

Perrin JM & MacLean WE (1988) Children with chronic illness: the prevention of dysfunction. *Pediatric Clinics of North America.*

Rogers CR (1977) *On Personal Power.* London: Constable.

Rogers CR (1983) *Freedom to Learn for the 80s.* Columbus, Ohio: Charles E Merrill.

Sabbeth BF & Leventhal JM (1984) Marital adjustments to chronic childhood illness: a critique of the literature. *Pediatrics.* Vol 73, No 6. pp. 762–768.

Numeric

1. Rogers CR. *Freedom To Learn for the 80s.* Columbus, Ohio: Charles E Merrill, 1983.

   · · · · · · · · · · · · · · · · ·

3. Ghazi F & Cook S. Monitoring research in a nursing college. *Nursing Standard.* Vol 7, No 47. 1993. pp. 27–30.

   · · · · · · · · · · · · · · · · ·

5. Perrin JM & MacLean WE. Children with chronic illness: the prevention of dysfunction. *Pediatric Clinics of North America,* 1988.

6. Sabbeth BF & Leventhal JM. Marital adjustments to chronic childhood illness: a critique of the literature. *Pediatrics.* Vol 73, No 6. 1984. pp. 762–768.

7. Pearce C. Formal measurement of pain by nurses. *Nursing Standard.* Vol 7, No 2. 1993. pp. 38–39.

8. Midence K, Davies SC & Fuggle P. Sickle cell disease: courage in the face of crisis. *Nursing Times.* Vol 88, No 22. 1992. pp. 46–48.

9. Knowles MS. *The Adult Learners: A Neglected Species.* 2nd edn. Houston: Gulf, 1978.

10. Abrams SJ. The self concept of sickle cell disease and their siblings and related maternal attitudes. *Dissertation Abstracts International.* Vol 47, No 10. 1987. p. 3869.

    · · · · · · · · · · · · · · · · ·

12. Graham, AV, Reed KG, Levitt C, Fine M & Medalie JH. Care of a troubled family and their child with sickle cell anemia. *Journal of Family Practice.* Vol 15, No 1. 1982. pp. 23–32.

13. Capelli M, McGrath PJ, MacDonald NE, Katsanis J & Lascelles M. Parental care and overprotection of children

with cystic fibrosis. *British Journal of Medical Psychology*. Vol 62, No 3. 1989. pp. 281–289.

. . . .

15. Lindeman E. *The Meaning of Adult Education*. New York: New Republic, 1926.

. . . .

18. Knowles MS. *The Modern Practice of Adult Education: From Pedagogy to Andragogy*. Chicago: Follett, 1980.

. . . .

27. Knowles MS. *Self Directed Learning: a guide for learners and teachers*. Chicago: Follett, 1975.

. . . .

29. Bird C & Hassall J. *Self-administration of drugs: a guide to implementation*. London: Scutari Press, 1993.

30. Rogers CR. *On Personal Power*. London: Constable, 1977.

ACTION

After reading the previous section, you should hopefully be able to find your way around your library. To complete this section, find the following journals:

- *Health Visitor.*
- *Nursing Standard.*
- *International Journal of Nursing Studies.*
- *Senior Nurse.*

What referencing styles do they use?

_____

_____

Are they full references?

_____

_____

As a result of working your way through this chapter, which of the two styles discussed do you prefer? Make a few brief notes.

_____

_____

_____

_____

BIBLIOGRAPHY

The bibliography at the end of a piece of work serves to show the reader the amount of reading you have done to substantiate your argument. The bibliography will not be a replica of your references because the reference section will include only works that have been quoted in the text, whereas the bibliography will include books that have not been cited in the text but which have enhanced your understanding of the subject.

8 CRITICALLY REVIEWING RESEARCH REPORTS

If you are required to review a piece of research by another writer, it is important to consider some questions that all researchers address when undertaking a project. This chapter will help you understand how to review critically a piece of research or an article so that you can decide whether an article will be beneficial to you in your research or study. You can also use this exercise to review an assignment or essay that you have done, which will give you a guide as to where there may be room for improvement.

It is very easy, when reviewing a paper, to be influenced by an author's style of writing, the journal in which the paper is published or the quality of the print, or you may simply disagree with some of the findings after an initial reading. This type of reading is referred to as *subjective*, whereas we should be attempting to develop a more *objective* approach.

To review articles critically, it is essential to read an article three or four times and consider the content by referring to some of the following headings:

(1) **Style**

- Is it easy to read, and are the arguments logically presented?

- Is it well presented, e.g. layout, graphics, etc.?

(2) **Relevance**

- Is the information relevant to the paper?

- Are all the issues correctly identified and addressed?

(3) Reading

- Does it appear that the author has read widely around the subject?

- Are all the references fully documented?

(4) Research

- Are the methods of research clearly identified and are they appropriate?

- Is there a clear explanation of the sample or population discussed in the report?

- Do the author(s) provide evidence of where and when the research was carried out?

(5) Analysis and discussion

- Are the discussion and the information relevant to the topic?

- Is the analysis clear?

- Are the arguments of the paper discussed in relation to work practice or policy in any way?

- Is the article likely to be of any benefit to the profession?

◼◼◼◼ ACTION

Read the 10 point checklist below and use this as a framework for critically reading a current research report or article of your choice.

Check the good and bad characteristics listed and tick A, B, C, D, depending on how you rate the article. For a fuller understanding of the grading system, see below.

Author and title of article:

_____

_____

GOOD CHARACTERISTICS	A	B	C	D	BAD CHARACTERISTICS
Style					
Clear, logical and unambiguous presentation					Badly written, too long or too short
Relevance					
Relevant issues					Issues not identified
Reading					
Evidence of wide reading					Inappropriate evidence
Full and accurate bibliography and referencing					Inaccurate and/or incomplete bibliography and/or referencing
Research					
Appropriate method(s) of research clearly identified					Inappropriate method(s) of research or insufficiently identified
Clear explanation of sample/population					Lacking explanation of sample/population
Evidence of where and when research was carried out					Insufficient evidence of where and when research was carried out
Analysis and discussion					
Discussion and material relevant to topic					Majority of discussion and material irrelevant to topic
Application of theory to practice					Minimal application
Clear analysis of relevant information					Unsupported value judgements and/or anecdotes

When you have completed your review, allocate 4 points for A, 3 for B, 2 for C and 1 for D. If you have managed to allocate a grade for each of the 10 points, total the score. The following grades can then be awarded:

A	31–40
B	21–30
C	11–20
D	10 or under

The grades might indicate the following:

Mostly A grade – a good article

The author(s) have critically evaluated facts, principles, theories and research relevant to the topic and have analysed and synthesised the facts.

Mostly B grade – work of a reasonable standard

The majority of the report is reasonably well presented. It generally shows clear evidence of the use of appropriate research methods for collecting and analysing data, and provides a lively argument.

Mostly C grade – a low standard report

The work may be presented in a format describing issues of theory and practice. However, it presents irrelevant evidence in the form of detailed and outdated facts, and does not define theory or practice in a comprehensive and systematic way. Some of the report may be illogical and incoherent, and it offers little in the way of conclusion and summary.

Mostly D grade – a poor article

The article may include serious errors or inaccuracies in the data or evidence given, which will raise serious doubts about the quality of the research. The report may omit major and basic data or findings that are central to recent progress on the research topic in question. The report will lack a high quality of presentation and will show no signs of appreciating academic arguments and referencing.

Having completed this section, you should now be more aware of what is required of a good research article and be able to follow the five steps set out at the beginning of section 6 when criticising a piece of research.

9 WRITING REPORTS

It is important for any report to be well laid out and well structured. If you wish to write a report based on a study you have undertaken, it is important to use a structure which is clear and easy to follow.

The following is a list of contents of a typical report. You may wish to use this list or rearrange it, depending on your own preferences.

(1)   Title, author, date.

(2)   Contents.

(3)   Terms of reference.

(4)   Introduction.

(5)   Evidence or data.

(6)   Findings.

(7)   Conclusions.

(8)   Recommendations.

(9)   References.

(10) Appendices.

Try using this as a structure for your first major report. You should consider this as a useful framework for structuring reports.

ACTION

Select two or three reports from your library and compare the structures or formats.

Which do you feel has the most impact and why?

_____

_____

_____

_____

_____

_____

_____

_____

_____

REPORT STYLES

What style should the report adopt?

- Use a style which is concise and straightforward.

- Be careful not to overgeneralise.

- Avoid jargon and acronyms.

- Be consistent in the use of the first or third person.

- If paraphrasing, be careful not to lose the meaning of another writer's work.

Always allow enough time to write a report, especially if you have deadlines to meet.

In your report aim for:

- Pleasing presentation
- Structure
- Focus
- Clarity
- Logic

10 DEVELOPING A PERSONAL ACTION PLAN

Having decided how well you have done in this workbook, and whether or not you need any further help, the following action plan can be used to help you structure what you do next.

Personal action plan

Date	What I need to achieve	What I need to do	Possible difficulties	Help available

To use the action plan:

(1) Date

Enter your starting date.

(2)   What I need to achieve

Enter the goals you need to achieve on a course or at work. Identify realistic goals which take you forward one step at a time.

(3)   What I need to do

For each goal, enter the action you need to take to achieve it.

(4)   Possible difficulties

Enter realistic challenges that might prevent you achieving your goal if not addressed.

(5)   Help available

Enter the name or position of the person or persons who can help you to overcome difficulties.

Your plan might look like this:

Date	What I need to achieve	What I need to do	Possible difficulties	Help available
26–2–93	Learn word processing skills	Find out about local courses	Time consuming, high costs	Local college or adult education centre

11 EVALUATING YOURSELF

How did you do?

- Very well.
- Well.
- Mediocre.
- Need much more help.

Having worked your way through this workbook, you should now have a much better understanding of self-directed learning and the way it works. It is important with this type of study that you should be able to assess yourself on how much of the course you have understood. Answer YES or NO to the three questions below to help you assess your own understanding of this workbook.

SAQ

(1) Can you undertake a course of study or a project and plan your work so that you will comfortably reach the completion date and finish the course or project without falling behind?

(2) Can you complete a literature search using the various services your local library has to offer?

(3) Are you confident that you can put together a comprehensive and well-structured research proposal and present it in a professional way?

In the introduction, it was explained that this workbook is intended as an introduction to self-directed learning and research. Having completed the workbook, you should feel confident enough to go on to further study.

It is suggested that your next step should be to undertake a small-scale study in a field of your own interest and to build upon the skills and knowledge outlined in this book.

12 BIBLIOGRAPHY

Apps JW (1982) *Study Skills for Adults Returning to School,* 2nd Edition. London: McGraw Hill.

British Standards Institution (1990) *Recommendations for Citing and Referencing Published Material* (BS 5605). London: BSI.

British Library (1950–) *British National Bibliography.* London: British Library.

Buzan T (1971) *Speed Reading.* Newton Abbott: David & Charles.

Buzan T (1982) *Use Your Head.* Revised Edition. London: BBC Publications.

Casey F (1993) *How To Study: a practical guide,* 2nd ed. London: Macmillan.

Charter S (1989) *Understanding research in nursing.* Geneva: WHO.

Clifford C & Gough S (1990) *Nursing Research: a Skills-Based Introduction.* Hemel Hempstead: Prentice Hall.

Codlin EM (1986) *Aslib's Shorter Directory of Information Sources in the United Kingdom,* 6th edn. London: Aslib.

Cohen L & Marion L (1980) *Research Methods in Education.* London: Croom Helm.

Commission on Nursing Education (1985) *The Education of Nursing: A New Dispensation,* (The Judge Report). London: RCN.

Cormack DFS (1991) *The Research Process in Nursing,* 2nd ed. Oxford: Blackwell.

Cox S (1987) Peer and self assessment: Study of methods used at Learning Systems Centre, Coventry Polytechnic. *Nursing Times*, Vol 8, No 33, 62–64.

De Leeuw M & De Leeuw E (1990) *Read Better, Read Faster*, 2nd ed. Harmondsworth: Pelican.

Dempsey DFS (1986) *The Research Process in Nursing*, 2nd ed. London: Jones & Bartlett.

Freeman R (1982) *Mastering Study Skills*. London: Macmillan.

Good M & South C (1988) *In the Know: 8 keys to successful learning*. London: BBC Books.

Harman CA (1984) *How To Study Effectively*. Cambridge: National Extension College.

Hills PJ (1980) *Effective Study Skills*. London: Pan.

Irving A (1982) *Starting to Teach Study Skills*. London: Edward Arnold.

Jarvis P (1985) *The Sociology of Adult and Continuing Education* (especially the introductory chapter). London: Croom Helm.

Knowles J (1970) *The Modern Practice of Adult Learning*. London: Croom Helm.

Last RWS (1986) *Making Sense of How to Study*. Dundee: Lochee Publications.

Marshall A & Rowland F (1983) *A Guide to Learning Independently*. Milton Keynes: Open University Press.

Mason S (1992) *Management: A Selected Bibliography*, Vol 15. Bradford: MCB.

Millard L & Tabberer R (1985) *Help Yourself To Study*. Harlow: Longman.

Northedge A (1990) *The Good Study Guide*. Milton Keynes: Open University Press.

Ogier M (1989) *Reading Research*. London: Scutari Press.

Open University (1979) *Preparing To Study*. Milton Keynes: Open University Press.

Open University (1979) Research Methods in Education and the Social Sciences. Course DE304, 3rd level. Milton Keynes: Open University Press.

Parsons C (1976) *How To Study Effectively*. London: Arrow Books.

Pollack L (1984) 6 steps to a successful literature search. *Nursing Times*, 31 October, pp. 40–43.

Rowntree D (1976) *Learn How To Study*, 2nd ed. London: Macdonald.

Royal College of Nursing (1972–) *Nursing Bibliography*. London: RCN.

United Kingdom Central Council for Nursing, Midwifery and Health Visiting (1986) *Project 2000: A New Proposition for Nurses*. London: UKCC.

Wainwright GR (1972) *Rapid Reading Made Simple*. London: WH Allen.

Walsh F (1985) *A Bibliography of Nursing Literature*. London: Library Association.

Watts MH (1988) *Shared Learning* (Royal College of Nursing Research Series). London: Scutari Press.

Wright DJ (1992) *Directory of Medical and Health Care Libraries in the United Kingdom and the Republic of Ireland*, 8th edn. London: Library Association.